THE INTENTIONAL LEADER

THE INTENTIONAL LEADER

A Practical Guide to Leadership Essentials New Edition

KIRSTEN BLAKEMORE

Sue Blakemore, Editor

Contents

Acknowledgments		1
Introduction		3
1	Trust	8
2	Wellness	16
3	Executive Presence	22
4	The New Norm	28
5	Diverse and Inclusive Mindset with Actions	34
6	Playing it Fair	38
7	Talk the Talk, Walk the Walk	44
8	Manage the Work	50
9	Build Your Bench	55
10	Create Team Cohesion	58
11	Be a Mentor, Find a Mentor	62
12	Confrontation Does Not Equal Battle	66

13	Manage Time or It Will Manage You	71
14	Change & Lead Strong	75

Acknowledgments

I am grateful to each of the employees and leaders I have worked with over the years. I learn from every situation I am in and have always held these experiences as invaluable.

We always have the opportunity to learn from each other. This is a belief I hold. I aim to share the best practices I have gleaned from working as a business leader, coach, consultant, group facilitator. As such, people have shared their successes and challenges in business with me and more importantly with other people. Because of their vulnerability and willingness to share, I can pass on these important lessons to my readers.

I could not have written this book (and the revision) without the patience of my Mom, the English teacher and editor. The way I write is simply to type my thoughts, points and other lessons without a thought of grammar. I then send to her and she will walk through each character adding her grammar and word smith-ing. I am grateful beyond words to my Mother, not only for her expertise but for her guidance and love.

With the shift to remote work many find building and maintaining relationships more difficult. What legacy do you want to leave? What do you want people to remember about you? The choices we make stay with us and define who we are. The ripple effect from the choices you make emanates impacting all that is around us, and beyond. It is also how people perceive us by the choices we make and how we hold ourselves.

Introduction

This first version of this book was written at the onset of the COVID-19 pandemic. The business world has since changed, as a result of the pandemic, the most obvious change in the workforce is the hybrid model. For many, a learning curve still pushes people to think differently about how they lead. We have been forced to change how we interact with people. For those that are extroverts, even the hybrid model can be difficult. These people thrive in a collective setting where they can brainstorm in a collaborative fashion. They are energized by being around people. For the introverts, the hybrid model presents other challenges. Surviving a day which consists of meeting after meeting without a break leaves them feeling drained of energy at the end of it all. Other challenges emerged that many have had to overcome. For example, how do you keep employees engaged, especially on video? How do you stay engaged working from home while managing multiple tasks, such as running a household and leading a business? How do you connect with your people now when you were used to connecting face to face? How do you check in on your employees without micromanaging? Finally, how do you keep productivity high when many are faced with new distractions at home – i.e. kids, partners also working from home, pets, etc... The principles that are discussed in the subsequent chapters are foundational and can be used with both remote and in-office employees.

Many employees are promoted into a managerial role for the technical skill they have honed over time. However, many lack the "soft skills" of managing people. I use the term soft skill only because it is a commonly known term with which people are familiar. The critical skills referred to in this book are "people skills" and are anything but soft.

I hear frequently this concern when working with Human Resources (HR) leaders. Some organizations just let the struggling manager's flail. Others put a time limit on the new managers for development before moving them back into their independent contributor role a "grace period."

Understand, that as a leader, you are always being watched. How you speak, react, and behave are under the scrutiny of those who work for you, above you and around you. In many cases, the position you left is still vacant; therefore, you may have that workload as well. Onboarding new hires can be time consuming so, not only do you have the pressure of completing the new workload you have been handed, but you are expected to know how to lead people, gain loyalty from your team, and take care of their needs, as well. Starting out in a new role is a heavy burden to bear. The typical expectation is that you can handle it. Just like being a new parent, you are given no manual to becoming a great manager within your particular role and with your specified dynamics and complexities. With the additional workload and extra pressure of being a new manager, time management is an ongoing challenge. It's easy to feel as though you are just keeping your head above water. And there are those who have been in managerial roles for a significant amount of time and still struggle to build a following. Perhaps you have had 360 results come back less than desirable and wondered what happened. The truth is that you can be in a C-suite or a new managerial role and have similar people challenges and interpersonal relationship conflict.

The good news is that the steps and tools detailed in this book can be readily applied as they are simple. Interestingly, they should be common sense. And yet, so many new managers do not make these steps and tools a common practice.

Use this guide as an awareness tool to self-assess. Many employees at all levels of an organization spend very little time in self-reflection. And yet, that is key to becoming a strong people leader.

As an executive coach and speaker, I work with groups in the professional world across all industries. A prevailing theme that arises is a common complaint; "they" have a problem or are not doing "their" work. If we would simply turn that statement inward and ask ourselves a few questions, to inspire self-reflection and thought, more companies would develop successful leaders. It's easier to look at others and see their faults. It's much harder for one to see their own potential traps.

The premise of the book is to recognize what outcomes you want to achieve. Whether in a common interchange or on a large project, do your actions assist you in achieving the desired outcome? At the end of each chapter there are self-reflective questions. The questions are intended to assist you in exploring your current mode of operating, what your intentions are, and what you desire the outcomes to be.

Allow me to provide an example of this process as it played out in an event with my son when he was in middle school. I was visibly upset when his teacher did not list any of his grades on the school's internal website so we could see them. Her inability to post his grades left us in the dark, not knowing if he were doing well, if he understood the material, if he was doing his work, or if the content were too easy. He said to me after seeing my dismay, "Mom, yell at her."

I thought about it. It might have temporarily felt good to yell at her, after seeing her email explaining all the reasons why she couldn't post grades. But I said to him, "What is the outcome we want to achieve here?"

He mentioned that he wanted to see his grades, and he was hoping they would be good. I added that I was hoping we could also make her an advocate for him. So, I asked if that was the outcome we desire, would yelling at her get us there? He knew the obvious answer.

There were other options we could take that would more likely obtain the outcome we hoped to achieve, and we discussed them. Ultimately, we took another path moving us a bit closer to our desired outcome. That process had us first checking ourselves to reflect on our emotional state.

A very common response is to allow emotion to dictate one's actions. It's reactive and many times we are left having to clean up a mess we made in our fury.

One of the most important aspects of this book is the guide at the end of each chapter; use it for reflection and direction. Reflect on your reactions to situations and consider what you want to achieve as a desired outcome. Direct your thoughts and actions in a proactive way which will support you achieving desired outcomes in those situations.

Included are quotes from leaders, who when asked, "What has made you a successful manager?" added their insights so that you can learn from others who have already walked this journey.

The intention of this straightforward guide is to shed light on several common mistakes you can avoid as well as actionable, simple steps to developing your leadership ability and interpersonal skills.

1

Trust

"A team is not a group of people that work together. A team is a group of people that trust each other." ~ Simon Sinek

Leadership is different from managing people. You can be a leader without managing people but have the natural ability to lead so that people will want to follow. So, what distinguishes good leadership from bad? Typically, for those of you who have been led by a "bad" leader, you know it (and could probably name them and the qualities that made their leadership bad). There are certain qualities that would justify the "bad" label: Being dishonest, disrespectful, unable to keep confidential information confidential, not practicing what you preach, demeaning employees with others on your team, gaslighting and taking credit for work that one of your employee's produced (just to name a few). We know bad leadership when we experience it, but how do you begin to cultivate strong, positive habits so that people appreciate your style of leadership? This book will provide a foundation for you to build the "soft skills" of leading people as well as practical principles.

To lay the foundation for this book, the first chapter is devoted to building trust by leading with love. Through contrast there is clarity. Let me explain: What I have found through my coaching work is when I say something like "lead with love" to my clients, it doesn't always resonate. But if when we discuss how it feels when they are taken off a reoccurring meeting without prior notice, not given a promotion they were promised, or when they have been manipulated by their manager or even worse gaslit, they understand what it feels like to be managed by fear. Hence, through contrast there is clarity. It is clear to my clients how it feels so badly to be managed by someone who is motivated by fear. They lead with a hidden agenda, trying to figure out how to get the upper hand and how to use people for their own gain even when it means lying or twisting the truth and putting their employee down publicly.

Leading from fear is coming from a mindset of lack. These are some examples of thought with an origin of fear:

- If I don't do everyone's work for them, I could look bad to my stakeholders and that would be costly. I have to micromanage them because I don't trust them. (Insert the truth: *I don't trust myself enough to allow my team to do their best work and coach them if it isn't up to par. The worst for me is having stakeholders really see who I am and realize that I don't know what I am doing and do not deserve my job or to be promoted.*)

- I cannot let anyone who works for me have the upper hand or appear to know more than I know. If they do, I will have to bring them down in meetings in front of others so everyone can see I am in control and I know more than everyone. (Insert truth: *I am afraid of not knowing everything I "should" know. If I am exposed, I could lose respect and my position of authority. If people find out others know more than I, then they may give them my job.*)

- I need all the power, and if someone shows an upper hand I will take them down. (Insert truth: *I am afraid to let go of control and empower my team, because that could make me look weak. If I look weak, I could lose my position of authority, and I could lose out on the promotion or worse be demoted. I also fear not being included in the executive clique if people find out I am not good enough.*)

- I cannot give honest feedback to people if it is anything less than good unless I have something to gain. (Insert truth: *I fear if I tell someone where they fell short and what they need to improve, I may hurt their feelings and then they won't like me. I need everyone to like me so I can continue to build networks which will strengthen my chances of promotion.*)

These are examples of fear-based leadership. I have led groups where we discuss what trust looks like and what it doesn't look like. The above are examples of what eroding trust by fear looks like. Indicators of lack of trust in a team are attrition, low morale and engagement, and lack of productivity just to name a few. Have you experienced a leader who leads with fear? If so, how did it make you feel? If you have had these experiences, and you remember how it made you feel, use this to inspire the opposite in your leadership practice.

Anytime you have an angry, jealous, negative, raging, lack, scarcity, fear-based thought, it's not love. It is fear leading, directing the thought patterns.

Trust is built when leaders lead with love. Examples of love-based leadership are employing empathy, vulnerability, openness and creating an inclusive environment. Recently I was leading a trust workshop. At the end of the workshop, the leader shared a very vulnerable message engaging his team and inviting them to meet him in a safe and open environment. It struck me profoundly that he went against the norm and opened his heart to his team. He modeled love-based leadership which creates an environment of trust.

At a separate workshop I led, the leader was working with her team and reviewing her SWOT analysis. As she was presenting to her team they suggested some additions. She stopped presentation mode and added their thoughts. This may seem small but the powerful non-verbal is *everyone is included in building the direction of the team.* She created a trusting, safe environment for people to share excitement and concerns not only in that moment but moving forward as well.

Is it possible to lead with compassion and sensitivity and still be effective and impactful? Think of it in terms *of how do I get it right* (love based mindset) instead of *how can I be right (fear based mindset.)*

At one point in business, it was a non-verbal rule that the workplace was not where you brought emotions or your personal self; those were left at home.

However, we are in the midst of a tremendous shift in the workforce dynamic. Employees are no longer tolerating poor leaders. In my experience, it is one of the main reasons people leave their current position. Now more than ever, leaders must lead with love and build trust within their team.

It is critical that we are able to personally connect with employees whether they work virtually or in person. When leading with love, what manifests is abundance, compassion, being in-service, joy, laughter, happiness, passion, and feeling good in knowing you are in that unbelievable creative state. As a leader, you have to intentionally lead with love and be aware when fear enters the picture. This requires constant self-analysis and awareness. Self-awareness is a commonly mentioned topic but unfortunately, not enough of us are truly aware in the moment.

When our reaction to any situation is to look inwards first, we will be able to manage and understand our thoughts and feelings. Understanding where our feelings originate, the thoughts we had leading us to feeling a specific way, can create a powerful pause in which our next move will not be one we regret. You may slip back into fear but use your awareness to inspect "where are you in this moment and what is motivating you?" Know, you can shift into love leadership when you're working with your team and leading your subordinates or your managers, even if you felt like fear had been your mode only moments before. Look for the indicators if you are not fully aware of your thoughts, feelings and motivations. If you are focused only on self, self-importance, and self-benefit then likely fear is the driver. The downside to this mindset is that other people could perceive you to be self-centered and lacking the awareness to truly support your team and have an "others" perspective.

Leading with love means you trust your intuition and understand that learning from experience is part of the process. Building on the negative and positive experiences, so you can continue to be intentional with your leadership, moving forward is wisdom in practice.

I have a client who demonstrated this type of leadership.

For months she worked for a boss who continuously reduced her, minimized her value and made promotion promises which were never kept. During our weekly meetings, she would share new experiences of her manager excluding her, gaslighting and reducing her scope. She questioned her value on many occasions and wondered if these hurt feelings were justified. Since she couldn't compare notes with anyone, she used coaching to talk about what she was experiencing. She had thoughts of getting back at her boss or leaving. We discussed many times what would her best self do in these moments? She wondered how she would find her voice in order to stand up for herself. It takes tremendous courage to come from love when you feel you are being victimized and marginalized. She did find her voice through sharing her feedback with her boss. It was a scary moment for her, but she did so with grace and courage. In a recent email, where she shared how an interchange with her boss contained more manipulation and fear, her comment to me was "when they go low, we go high." It was a powerful moment where her choice was clear: she chose to lead with love and not to retaliate out of fear.

Self-Reflection Questions:

- What leaders have made a positive impact in my life? Did they lead with fear or love?
- What examples of their leadership stood out?
- Have you modeled that behavior as well?
- What is important about your leadership that will define you to others?

2

Wellness

"When "I" is replaced with "we" even illness becomes wellness."
~ Malcom X

Before launching into the tactical list of what steps you can take to experience wellness more frequently, it is important to note that as a leader, you model wellness for not only your team but for others with whom you interact. If you are answering emails at 11:00PM, then you send the signal this is the norm you expect from yourself and others. This schedule leads to burnout.

Of course, there are exceptions where fires need to be put out and you may need to send the occasional email in the wee hours of the morning, but this is the exception and not the rule. I cannot share how many times clients have said their managers work nights and weekends so that they feel the pressure to do the same. As one of my clients said: "I can't hear you, your actions are speaking to loud." Your actions model what you expect.

Burnout leads to attrition risks. Wellness is an area that many companies are tracking to ensure they are retaining top talent. Your role is to clarify a positive expectation which models a healthy level of wellness, so you retain your people.
There are three parts to wellness that I will highlight here. They are physical, mental, and emotional.
Physical wellness sounds simple: get 30 minutes of aerobic activity a day (at least). Eat healthy, well balanced, small frequent meals.

In the remote world, we can sit at our desk on video, meeting after meeting and before we know it the day is over (and we may or may not have eaten.). I have had days where my meetings are 8-4 straight with no breaks built in. It is not my norm and if I find myself in that situation, I will conclude my meetings a few minutes early to take my bio breaks and have my snacks or food at my desk. I also take stand up breaks (or stretching) to circulate my blood flow. The common occurrence I hear from my clients is many of them struggle with overwhelm or drain at the end of a day of video meetings. The ideal is to balance or interject your video meetings with phone calls instead and perhaps add a walk and talk meeting as well. Since the pandemic started, we now have built in assumptions that if we are having a meeting, it will be on video. We must request a phone call meeting!

Those who work in an office as well or full time have the benefit of walking to a meeting or seeing people in the hallways to break up the day with conversation. These helpful breaks are needed to energize us and keep up our stamina.

Regardless, building exercise in before, during or after work is a way we can give back to our bodies. During the workday, it's ideal to take a walk throughout the day (even a quick walk around the block) to encourage the blood and oxygen flowing.

The food we eat is important to our energy levels throughout the day. If we eat a heavy meal, then sit all day to work, we do not support our bodies in an optimal response. Limiting the sugar and fat (i.e. fast food fat) intake will help to give us longer term energy. These are all rules of thumb rather than an all or none. It's about balance. On the other hand, if we are so busy through the day that we neglect to eat at all, that does not fuel our bodies and minds to accomplish, an optimal operating level.

The last part of the wellness is the mental and emotional wellness. When you work with or for people who are toxic leaders, this can lead to your expending a tremendous amount of energy thinking about what they mean, how it will impact you and what will happen as a result. I hear frequently how conflicts impact people's emotions and the thinking starts to become the equivalent to being on a hamster wheel. You can perseverate on the *he said she saids* and it can become excessively draining. You can lose motivation towards work and your drive to accomplish.

I have a client who works in crisis. Her daily routine is to handle traumatic situations. She is balanced, thoughtful and really excels in her work. However, what drains her completely is when she is put in the position of questioning the motives and behaviors of her leader. She has to determine when he is hazing her, gaslighting, excluding her or simply setting her up to fail. She is brilliant in crisis, but not when it becomes a personal afront. It is draining and all-consuming.

Now, ask yourself what kind of leader you are. If you have ever experienced a leader who leads with fear - gaslighting, manipulating, lying, power trips, and micromanaging - then you know how awful it feels. It is draining. It leads to thinking about "is it me" questions, it's both isolating and devaluing. There is a shelf life for how long one will tolerate it. And if you have experienced it, then you can use that experience to ensure you never lead that same way. You will know that leading with fear breeds toxicity. We are just talking about the energy expenditure here. But the stress these situations can have on one's body is significant. I know people who endured these stressful situations which led to autoimmune disorders, strokes, hives, and migraines, to name a few.

Your mindset is determined by you. When you are not intentional, your mindset can lead to undesirable outcomes. I highly recommend spending some time each day in meditation. Whether it's with using an app like Calm or Headspace, or just experience time alone focused on "be-ing", these valuable to your well-being. I start each day with this practice, focused on being grateful. For me, this practice creates a positive, open mindset. Science has demonstrated the power of meditation. If that is of interest to you, I strongly recommend Dr. Joe Dispenza's work (https://drjoedispenza.com.)
Unless you intentionally devote time to this practice, it is usually the first to drop off the list of items to accomplish in the day. You choose your thoughts, actions and emotions every day. Having time to center yourself is a sure way to be responsive rather than reactive throughout your day, no matter what obstacles you encounter.

Self-Reflection Questions:

- What areas need my focus to increase health and well-being?
- What am I modeling to my people about wellness?
- Do I have opportunities to communicate more on the importance of wellness to my people?
- Am I building into my team a structure of trust and compassion?

3

Executive Presence

"We communicate much more through our presence than the words."
~ Sri Sri Ravi Shankar

These two words, *executive presence*, have become common in the business world vernacular within the last several years. In coaching, I have many clients seeking more of this in their leadership. What I also hear is that executive presence varies in meaning to a wide variety of people. Here are some of the most common desired traits: confidence, constructing brief narratives (both written and verbal), fearlessly to say "I *don't know*" when they really don't, and to have a solid presence when public speaking.

Confidence: What I have realized is that confidence is the foundation for all other traits. The Oxford Dictionary defines confidence as a feeling of self-assurance arising from one's appreciation of one's own abilities or qualities. Furthermore, confidence comes from the Latin word 'fidere' which means "to trust"; therefore, having self-confidence is having trust in oneself.

In application:

- A belief in oneself to handle any situation they encounter.
- Self-awareness to know when their inner critic is telling them they are not good enough, smart enough, skilled enough and they reframe that thinking to support mindful decision making. Without that awareness, the inner critic (those critical, negative, self-deprecating messages we tell ourselves, whether you are conscious of them or unconscious) can direct our outward appearance and how people perceive us. I have heard it is difficult to have confidence when you are in a new role. True, and when you are open to learning and secure with not knowing everything, this can come across as self-assurance. This is the first step in building confidence. Eventually that comes when you feel comfortable in the situations in which you find yourself because you have had these experiences numerous times.
- Trust in yourself and others. You trust yourself to make

the best decisions. You are also open to making mistakes and do not feel the need to hide in shame but rather use as a learning mechanism.

Engaged: Whether you are a leader on video or in person, it is important to give people your full attention. How many times have you been on video and seen your audience checking their phones, pings, chats and emails while in conversation? It's distracting. While many fool themselves into believing they can multitask, we see your eyes and energy and can tell you are not fully present. This lack of full presence and engagement conveys the non-verbal "you are not as important to me as the other things I am doing."

Having executive presence also means you are fully present with your audience or the person with whom you are speaking. If you have an urgent matter arise, then communicate that and ask for time out. That would be preferable to having you pretend you are listening but really are distracted.

Communication: Executive presence with regards to communication is the ability to speak clearly and articulate the points. Many people find this easy when they are in 1:1's or in low pressure settings. But this skill can decline in meetings with stakeholders and people of influence. In these settings, some people process out loud when addressing a question to which they are unsure of the answer, and it may sound like they are rambling. If this is in an important meeting, then this response in undesirable. Further, learning to be concise in both emails and verbally is important. Clients have shared they would like to enhance their public speaking skills so their nerves do not distract them from conveying their message well. This trait is one that you can learn by taking a writing class, practicing speaking in groups like Toastmasters, and having learning tools to apply.

One tool that many of my clients have found useful is bullet pointing their thoughts in meetings in which the audience does not inspire added pressure. Verbally when they process what they want to say, they tell the story in a 1, 2, 3 framework. It has been helpful for a few of my clients to begin this process by writing their emails with this format. Telling a story in a bullet point fashion helps the listener follow your train of thought from beginning to end. After writing in this way, then begin to use this framework in your meetings and 1:1's, again with low pressure. The reason for the starting point of low pressure is simply to allow the process to flow without the potential invasion of the inner critic which always escalates the situation.

One of my clients would watch the news and bullet point out what he heard just to learn the flow of this style of communication. Regardless of the approach, ask for feedback so you know where you are advancing the skill and where you want to improve. Feedback is helpful in all of these cases as leaders continue to refine their communication skills.

The final point is regarding the energy you embody when it comes to your leadership. Your energy has a significant impact on your executive presence. Think of observing leaders who walk into a room full of people. Without knowing who they are, you still know they are in charge. It's the energy or non-verbal communication which conveys that message.

Your energy or presence may communicate fear as you begin an uncomfortable conversation, and it may communicate confidence that you own the room as you are about to speak. People feel it, they can read it (with or without knowing they are reading it).

Have you ever walked into a room where a couple had been fighting but stopped the moment you entered? You felt it strongly with all of your being, and uncomfortably exited the room. That is reading the energy. Your energy conveys your inner state. Mind your energy before going into a meeting or an important conversation. Have an awareness of what you are thinking and feeling. Thoughts and feelings create your energy. If you are having thoughts such as "I got this!" your feelings are likely that of confidence. On the other hand, thoughts such as "what if I make a mistake, ruin the presentation or worse, don't know an answer they ask me?" then it's likely these feelings are based on self-doubt, shame, and fear. You are diminishing your worth before you even enter the room, and that will be present in your energy. If this is not common practice for you to assess your thoughts and feelings in this way, which in turn affect your energy, a leadership coach can help.

Self-Reflection Questions:

- What areas are impacting my executive presence?
- What indicators do I have that point to needing more?
- Are there specific circumstances or people where you feel less confident and comfortable? What is the inner critic telling you? What is a helpful reframe?

4

The New Norm

"As we look ahead into the next century, leaders will be those who empower others."

~ Bill Gates

For those who have not had to lead within a virtual environment, this shift to a hybrid workstyle can be challenging. Even for those of us who have been remote before COVID, it can still be a challenge. The remote workforce is the new norm, and it is unlikely to return to the way it was. The following are basic guidelines with which to lead.

As a leader, you want the highest level of engagement,

productivity, and inspiration from your people. But the "old way" of managing may not be working.

So, let's look at engagement first (we discussed this in the previous chapter on Executive Presence because it reflects on you as a leader.) Engaged employees are focused on the work at hand. They do their job well and maybe even look toward upward momentum in their career path. But to be engaged, they must be included. Diverse and inclusive mindsets and behaviors are critical now more than ever. If you have ever been, or witnessed, the effects of being excluded from work or projects, then you know how damaging it can be. I worked for an organization where the leaders continued to use the same people who were similar to them in background and pedigree. After years of this behavior going unchanged (although complaints were made frequently) the company experienced high turnover, a drop in morale and less engagement from those still employed. The company's results were impacted by this behavior, and the employees were resentful and disengaged. There was little trust in leadership and very few took them seriously. The result was extremely detrimental to this company.

To foster engagement, one must be inclusive of all employees, not only a few. People leaders must recognize if they have a disposition to behave in an excluding way; then they must seek feedback around this topic to prevent repeating it. The question to ask oneself, "Where are my biases that may impact the way I lead?" We all have biases, but not all of us seek to understand the impact on others.

Instilling inclusivity engages people. This pandemic is said to bring out the best and the worst in people. Therefore, be mindful of your limitations and seek input as to where you can engage your people more thoroughly.

Productivity is higher when employees are recognized and engaged. Recognize your employees frequently. This is important in any work environment but crucial in a remote workforce. One way to keep your employees productive is to create fun meetings; use your sense of humor. I know fun and work typically do not go together but they should. When employees are having fun doing their work, their mindset is positive. This positive mindset encourages productivity and innovation. If you have ever been in a situation which is (or seen someone who is) negative at work and unhappy, their productivity wanes. On the flipside, when people are happy, laughing, and having fun, they are more productive. Research shows the "feel good" hormones endorphins are released through laughing, affecting our physiological state. (https://www.medicalnewstoday.com/articles/317756)

A leader admitted to me that she didn't know how to connect with her people now that she looks at them through a computer. She said she just couldn't seem to reach her people the way she used to.
In this case, I suggested looking at the background in the

person's house and bring up something as a point of conversation to get to know her people better.

When I was speaking to a new employee I said, "I see you have a guitar behind you, do you play?" He started telling me about his passion allowing me to know him better.
In portrait paintings of famous people, the painter typically included an item designating in what way that person was important. Look for what they find important.

Being virtual requires us to connect differently. We are forced to change the way we used to connect with our people because we are remote. At first, it may require more energy, thought and creativity. When we focus on the person and their interests, we can begin to build the bridge. As a quick example of how to create fun, a leader can have a board on SharePoint where the team members can answer personal questions, such as, "What is your favorite song or food?" At the end of the week the team can guess who wrote what.

It's a fun game that provides interesting personal information about each member of the team. This is a time to get to know your team. What do they enjoy outside of work? What's important to them personally? When employees feel like you care, they are more engaged, loyal, and more productive.
Finally, how do we inspire in a remote setting? Inspiration comes where there is connection, recognition, and spontaneity. Employees are remote but still want to develop and move

up the ladder in their career. Being remote can make it more difficult to see the impressive work people are doing. But our employees still want visibility and success. Therefore, the need to creatively provide opportunities to be seen for the work they do is critical. It may seem less organic than when we were in the office, but the need is still present.

Create open hours or coffee chat to see what people are working on and create the space on Zoom (or whatever platform you use) for people to share their work. We learn from each other. Since we cannot walk down the hall to a colleagues' office, we have to create the space to have visibility. You don't need to dedicate hours to this project, but you could label it a brainstorming hour where members of the team are sharing ideas and showing what others are doing. This time will not only inspire but foster more creativity. This is only one example of how you can create visibility for your team.
The point is to be inclusive and intentional.

Self-Reflection Questions:

- What might make my leadership more successful working with remote employees?

- Are my meetings dragging on? Are some team members "checking out"?
- What are some ways in which I can create connection with my employees?
- Do I have a connection with all of my employees or only a select few?
- Do I know what motivates them? Do I need to inquire about how they may be handling the new norm personally?

5

Diverse and Inclusive Mindset with Actions

"Love is the only force capable of transforming an enemy to a friend."
~Martin Luther King Jr.

A colleague of mine had once worked for an organization where the leadership team was homogenous: Same gender, race and religion. She was different, and she was consistently overlooked when it came to being assigned important projects by the leaders. She began questioning her value and worth.

She asked for feedback, and they said she was "good." Even after mentioning this concern to the leaders, nothing changed. Since it impacted her pay, she decided she would look elsewhere to work and gave her notice. During her exit interview, she told HR that she was tired of the discrimination and bias. Later that week, she received a call from one of the leaders telling her she was wrong, he was not biased. There was no way he was because he teaches about bias.

Unfortunately, we all have biases. One researcher said, if you have a brain, you have a bias. So as a leader it is up to you to have an open mindset to your blind spots. Get curious and request feedback to make certain you address those areas. Some member of your team is likely to notice one of your biases. So, don't despair! This will keep you honest. Building a diverse and inclusive team will create the environment to allow for differences. Ultimately, you must be open to the difference and understand you are modeling that acceptance for others.

Identify where you can become more inclusive with your team members. If you have adopted a new team, you may be unaware of the biases they have suffered in the past or the flagrant disregard for their individuality. In other words, you could be walking into a hornet's nest. This is where you leverage your curiosity to heal. As a leader you direct the importance of diversity of people and thought. If you can change your mindset, you'll be able to change your team dynamics.

Look at your team and the ideas that are generated. Are

they diverse or are your people and ideas similar? Be an observer in your meetings, your one-on-ones to notice if you are emphasizing difference as a benefit.

Too often we are so caught up with leading, we forget to observe. Look for ways of pointing out your observations so you're sharing these with others on your team. By modeling this behavior, you are telling them implicitly that observation is important and you are looking for ways of diversifying ideas, your talent pool and possible solutions.

As you continue to build your team and seek new talent to fill open roles, push to find quality candidates that will build difference in your team. Many studies reinforce differences pushes our boundaries to think conceive and innovate more. Sales and revenue have been shown to increase when we embrace difference and unique perspectives and people.

We tend to think of diversity and inclusion as an HR initiative but far from it. Each person has a role in leading the change, and as a leader you have a spotlight on you. Create D&I (diversity and inclusion) best practices. At every meeting, ask for a completely different out of the box solution to a problem. Invite all voices to be heard, and value their ideas. That doesn't mean you will have to implement all ideas, but it does mean you acknowledge and value their input.

Avoid being the leader in my story who believed he was

above bias. As a leader, look for ways of improving your understanding of bias and diversity. Actively seek to include every person, not just some people or the same people over and over. If you receive feedback that you are not inclusive or diverse in some way, you have the power to change. How you react to the feedback is critical in the message you send to your team. Your reaction will either build trust or erode.

Instead of getting angry, change your mindset from the problem to a focus on the solution. You need to look at this as an opportunity to change any type of negative beliefs or discrimination that may be occurring instead of allowing yourself to become defensive. With this mindset, you will find solutions to improve your leadership and create an inclusive diverse culture.

Self-Reflection Questions:

- Do you tend to choose the same people because they are efficient, and they work well with you?
- A peer shares with you feedback that has been circulating. People believe you shut down conversation and ideas that are different from your own. What do you do?
- What best practices can you create to foster open dialogue when people are offended or hurt?
- How diverse is your team?

6

Playing it Fair

"Equality is giving everyone a shoe. Equity is giving everyone a shoe that fits." Unknown

In my first management role, I learned a valuable lesson, one that has informed my actions in every subsequent position I have held. It has had such a tremendous impact on the way I lead, that this lesson is woven throughout every chapter.

Years ago, in my first management role I was promoted to assistant manager in a sales organization. My boss, who served as my teacher, was the manager of a national brand. We had just under 40 salespeople reporting to us. I gained many insights from my mentor; but one lesson was unintended and unfortunate.

I frequently heard from many on the team who felt the standards varied based on who the manager's favorites were. It wasn't fair and they were looking to me to rectify. As a person in a new role, I wanted to be a sponge, to absorb and learn.

But I quickly found out that my team wanted me to intervene when they felt wronged, and that happened all too often. I would spend quite a bit of time listening to the complaints. I noticed the impact these complaints had on their engagement and morale. The more they felt inequity, the more disengaged and/or grumbly they became. I would witness team members chatting quietly about the inequity, and when I would walk into the room, they would stop talking. It created a competitive environment filled with resentment and low morale.

This is what happens when managers exclude certain people, when their bias blinds them.

When my mentor left the company, I was promoted into her role. I knew the first order of business was to create a level playing field where people knew everyone would have the same expectations. I have taken that standard and applied it wherever I have worked, even now, some twenty years later.

Set clear expectations for your team members to ensure you have that same standard for all. If you provide exceptions for one, you set the expectation that you will waffle when it comes to holding people to any standard. If there is a valid reason to waffle, you may need to interpret that for the rest of your team so the message you send is that the particular exception is acceptable. The non-verbal message here is that if this same reason comes up for any team member, then that team member will also have a pass because you have accepted it in one case, and thus will accept it for all.

If there is no interpretation for the team, and the members learn of the incident (and they always do), then they will fill in the missing information. When there is missing information but no explanation, people typically fill that gap with their own narrative. That narrative is usually negative.

For example, Joe was put in charge of a project. He was a bit behind schedule but thought he would be able to meet the deadline anyway. However, Bob, Joe's colleague, told him that their manager gave the project to Bob to lead. Without a prior discussion between the manager and Joe, Joe is left wondering why that happened. He starts to fill in the missing information with possibilities such as, "My boss didn't think I could handle it. The important projects always go to Bob. Bob is his favorite." None of those could be accurate or they could all be. The point is the manager did not discuss the move with Joe. At that moment, Joe was simply filling in the missing information with his own narrative and it was negative.

Situations like this happen frequently. It is so simple to

assume the worst but a classic case of what not to do in a management role.

In this dynamic, one could easily point to Joe's problem of assuming the worst, but this leads us back to the manager's responsibility.

Think of how Joe's assumptions could have been avoided. Step 1: The manager speaks with Joe and after a discussion decides Joe will handle the project. Or alternately, Joe concedes he is struggling and could use Bob's help. Then, Step 2: the team is notified in a short meeting that Joe and Bob will be leading in a collaborative approach to complete the project on time.

This is an example of how a manager can prevent both favoritism as well as avoiding a team member filling in the gaps of missing information with their own negative narratives.

A common complaint that spreads across teams is the scheduling challenge. It may be scheduling breaks and it may be dealing with employee tardiness. I once had an employee who would clock-in and then stand in the kitchen getting coffee and chatting for long periods of time. The matter was brought to my attention as unfair. This employee was using company time to socialize in the kitchen and she was not doing her work. Thus, her work fell onto others to pick up the slack. As soon as I learned of this, I had to swiftly communicate go-forward expectations and how her current behavior would not meet those. We had a professional, kind conversation that ended with the desired outcome.

Any favoritism that occurs is detrimental to the morale of the company. As a manager you have a responsibility to uphold fairness within your team. Fairness includes the experiences you are creating for the employees and how they may interpret your decisions.

When moving into a managerial role, ask the individuals you will be managing, "What did the previous manager do well and what would like to see more of or done differently?" This will provide you with insight into what success looks like to your team, and what they expect from you as their manager.

Self-Reflection Questions:

- Do you have the same standards for all the individuals who work for you?
- Are there opportunities to fill in missing information with your workers?
- Are there situations where you need to interpret your actions for your people?
- You are faced with a situation in which your employee feels they have been dealt a poor hand. How do you lead through this with love and not fear?

7

Talk the Talk, Walk the Walk

"There is a difference between being a leader and being a boss. Both are based on authority. A boss demands blind obedience; a leader earns his authority through understanding and trust."
~Klaus Balkenhol

I have seen all too often the effects on new managers taking on the responsibility of management. With the abundance of work that comes with the new job can come a feeling of being overwhelmed. It's easy to focus on what's in front of you only in an attempt to complete all your work. The result may keep you separate from your team. Ultimately, your separation from the team can begin to create silos. There are too many silos today which prevent the highest level of success. The priority has to be to talk with your people frequently.

One successful leader I know has committed to weekly 1:1's with each member of her team, and she never fails to have them. Because she has made these meetings important, she has built strong individuals who think critically about their work. They have loyalty for their leader, who makes time for them, no matter what.

The challenge I hear frequently from employees is that their managers don't listen. The manager truly does not hear them. This may be a result of doing too much with too little time and not making the conversations with the individuals on their teams a priority. It is easy to let that slip first.

It may appear a report for an executive or a presentation for an initiative is more important than checking in with your team. But the truth is that you must build strong relationships with your team so that in times of challenge, they are with you and will back you. That is how you create loyalty. (And by the way, your people very likely want to be utilized and feel of value.)

Know your people. What motivates them? Why are they doing what they are doing? I remember years ago; I had an employee who reported to me and was known for her ability. She had been doing the job for years. She was an expert and people from other companies in similar roles would call asking for her help. She was that good.

I had just started as a new manager to the department. I was impressed by her knowledge. She was so good I thought she deserved a promotion. I actually had the whole plan laid out in my head and knew how I would help to accomplish it. When I finally asked her what success would like for her, she shared her dream of staying in her current role until she retired some ten years from that time. I was shocked. Literally, it was a mouth dropping moment. While I had a plan for her future, I quickly realized that I had no idea what motivated her. I didn't know her motivation for coming to work everyday with high engagement and a pride in the work she produced. It was a crucial piece of information that I lacked. When I spent time with her, I learned more about what she wanted, and that made me better able to help her achieve what was important to her.

The key here is to make time to connect with your people. It doesn't have to be time consuming but have a plan to understand the "why" for your people. They will respect you for making them a priority. They will feel more connected to you. Over time the connections you have created will produce loyalty.

The other half of this coin is walking-the-walk. If you expect a behavior or action from your people, for example, responding to emails in a timely fashion, then you must model that behavior. There is a big difference between a good and a poor manager.

Recently a woman in business development shared with me challenges which may cause her to leave her job. The company she worked for hired a new manager to lead her department. He told her and others that although he has no experience in this field, he is untouchable because he is in a protected class. He is using his diversity to strong-arm the company.

She complained that he never responds to her emails, but then complains that she is not doing her job. She has pleaded with him to make time for her so she can determine the direction on her projects with his help since he is the manager. Yet, he continues to be unresponsive.

Subsequently, a customer divulged a complaint about him. She struggled to know how to handle it. Bottom line was that she didn't want her manager to retaliate against her in any way. If he found out she was speaking about him to his supervisors, she could only imagine retribution would easily occur. After a struggle, she finally told his leader, resulting in no change. It was a serious complaint and the leaders did nothing. She is so miserable with him as her manager that she is considering leaving a job with a company that she loves. The company thus would lose a solid employee simply because a manager made poor decisions.

The impact this manager has had on her has not only affected her morale but her engagement in her job. She lost faith in leadership's ability to lead. This type of "poor" manager story is not isolated, unfortunately. It happens frequently. We don't know whether the leaders are handling this manager with discretion or not at all. But we do know they have not conveyed their reaction to the situation with the employee. Thus, her experience is that the leaders allow reckless behavior to persist without consequence.

The above story is a prime example of what can happen under poor leadership. It is equally important when a manager has a clear, strong sense of right and wrong and is driven to take the right approach. That has a powerful impact.

You always have a choice. As a manager, your people are always watching you. Be deliberate and make the right choices. Be led by high ethical standards which enable you to build trust with your employees because of your standards.

Again, as a leader you are always being watched. If you tell your people, for example, "We need to get this project done, so I am asking everyone to stay an hour later than their shift" but then you leave on-time, you will not earn the respect of your team. You must do as you say. In the same way, if you ask your team not to gossip, and you cut it off when it happens in meetings or around you, you are setting the example you have requested from your people. It may sound simple, and yet I hear this as a common complaint from employees. "I will do it when he or she does it," while they point their finger upwards alluding to their leadership.

Talking-the-talk means you consistently and frequently connect with your people. This approach includes actively listening and providing directive coaching. Walking-the-walk means your behavior role-models what you ask of your team.

Self-Reflection Questions:

- Are you meeting with your people on a regular basis?
- Are your ethical standards where you want them to be?
- Do you model the behavior you want your people to adopt?
- You learn people on your team think you choose favorites. In other words, you include the same people to do the work each time. How do you choose to handle it?

8

Manage the Work

"Great things are not done by one person. They're done by a team of people."
~Steve Jobs

In a meeting with an HR Manager, we discussed the developmental levels of her managers. She complained that newly hired managers came to their new role thinking they could delegate all their work. On the other side of the pendulum, some managers feel compelled to do the work themselves. In their minds, they ensure the work will be done on time and to their standards if they take on that burden. Of course, the latter approach of doing all of the work oneself will lead to burn out.

Neither of the extremes will add value to you as a manager. Those managers who want to take on all the work to ensure it is done correctly, end up adding tasks to their to-do list, which leads to never enough falling off. You end up spending long hours trying to keep your head above water. You may even work into personal time and spend weekends trying to complete it all. This is a short road to burnout.

If a manager delegates a majority of the work, one possibility is that the team builds resentment towards that manager.

Finding the balance can be a challenge for some new managers. With a heavy workload, it is easy to be seduced into canceling your 1:1's with your team. But, in the long run, it will prove detrimental not only to you but to your team.

Several of my clients have shared they are stick to a practice they were taught by their manager. They have weekly 1:1's with their people as well as monthly all-staff meetings. Furthermore, they have built in coffee chat or fireside chat office hours where anyone can show up during a two-hour span of time. These leaders are making themselves available for their people. They understand and prioritize their people and team. The non-verbal to the individuals on their team is "you are important and your growth is a priority to me."

The following qualities produce intentional leadership:

- Show humility; be approachable.
- Listen, listen, and listen again to your team.
- Ask probing questions – teach your team to ask probing questions.
- Be candid with each member of your team.
- Face challenges head on.
- Develop a strategy that can be executed.

This approach will give you a greater capacity to complete the projects you set out to execute in a timely manner because you have a team supporting your efforts.

When managing the workload, one must ask what tasks are most important to complete. Priorities tend to shift frequently. If there is confusion around what must be done, versus what would be nice to get done, speak with your leader. Then determine who on your team needs to be involved in the work. This is an opportunity for building your team and coaching them on the work they do as well as how they complete it.

It is very easy to fall into the trap of not trusting your team to do their work accurately. If this happens, you may choose to hover, aka micromanage. No one appreciates micromanagement and it will not earn trust. By doing this you send a non-verbal message that you do not trust in the quality or timeliness of their work. Be careful not to mistake coaching for micromanaging your people and their work.

You may be concerned that if you do not have your hand in every aspect of the work, then you will not make a good impression as a new manager. At this point, you may not know individual team members, while you have been given a role in which your work outcomes are in the spotlight. So, it's logical to want to ensure that the work that is produced by your team is worthy of the spotlight.

Beware of the trust trap. If you fail to take the appropriate steps to build trust among your workers, ultimately, you will lack trust in your team. To avoid falling into this trust trap, set clear expectations for your team's work. Then continue those conversations as you move through your projects. Your people should understand exactly what you want and the outcome you hope they produce. If they do not perform as you desire, revisit, and clearly articulate your expectations until there is a mutual understanding.

Self-Reflection Questions:

- Are you at one end of the pendulum? Do you delegate with an even distribution?
- Do you trust your team to complete their work accurately?
- What would they say if asked, "Does your manager trust you?"
- Do you have a belief that each of your team members can produce quality, on-time work? If not, what conversation do you need to have with those individuals?

9

Build Your Bench

"To build a strong team, you must see someone else's strength as a complement to your weakness and not a threat to your position or authority."
~Christine Caine

As you groom your employees to develop, you will gain from their contributions. Have the mindset to develop the individuals on your team so that at some point, if need be, they could replace you. It's a scary proposition for some but the right path to lead. Ultimately, you will be noticed for the team in which you have invested.

Leo Pranitis, Chief Commercial Officer at Mavrik Dental Systems says this about building a team:

*"Simply put, being a successful manager means you have to get the best **out** of others, rather than being the best **among** others. It requires that you pivot from your previous role as an individual contributor, and instead operate as though you are standing behind your team, guiding, advising, listening, coalescing, and supporting. This is one of the most significant factors that new managers neglect to acknowledge in the early days of their new journey, and frankly, most companies' training programs don't address it effectively either."*

The manager should put forth the effort to create opportunities for team building activities. This can impact the connections and the level of trust among the members of the team. Some organizations invest in outside companies hosting team building activities to immediately impact the team, break down barriers, and work effectively together. Your first meeting with the team is a prime opportunity to lay the foundation for a cohesive team with a sense of camaraderie.

For example, one team leader I met had each employee on her team write down on a piece of paper something they had done that no one knew. They handed in their paper and everyone had to guess who did what. It was a fun guessing game that brought the team closer together.

You may find that some individuals on your team have strengths in leading virtually. Find out by asking who is comfortable with leading Zoom or Google Meet Video type meetings and notice who on your team really shines while many are working remotely. This may be a great opportunity for you to empower the people on your team to stretch their responsibility.

Building your team means that you have moved the focus off of you and onto them. You are constantly thinking of creative ways to get the best from them. You are making decisions with the team in mind instead of only yourself. Successful managers move the focus from "me to we."

Self-Reflection Questions:

- Are you doing what you can to get the best out of the individuals on your team?
- What could you do differently that would raise them to the next level of success?
- Do you believe the individuals on your team could move into your role?
- You have an employee that wants a promotion, placing them in a different department. The role opens and they have been offered the promotion but that would require you to sign off on the employee's departure leaving you with an open headcount. You have more work than you can handle now and that opening will leave you overwhelmed. What do you do?

10

Create Team Cohesion

*"Our goals can only be reached through the vehicle of a plan.
There is no other route to success."*
~Pablo Picasso

Ensuring your team members are aligned and moving in the right direction may sound easy, but it is not frequent practice. The larger the team, the more difficult it is to galvanize the members to move towards their common goals. This starts with knowing what the organization needs to achieve by year-end. Then narrow the overarching goals to the appropriate level for your department. Now, decipher what your department needs to produce. Then, in turn, add the overarching goals of the organization to ensure the alignment.

Leo Pranitis adds:

"You must work to develop an intimate understanding of the goals for the company. As strategic plans and growth tactics cascade down through the organization to you for execution, it's now your responsibility to make them reality."

How do you accomplish that? Well, an almost sure-fire way to fail as a new manager is to assume that because you're in charge, people will automatically do what you tell them, blindly, without challenge. There is a significant difference between being a boss and creating "followership." A boss barks orders without explaining what the rationale is behind them. Followership dictates that you explain the plan, gain consensus, and buy-in, ensuring that everyone understands. A boss assigns blame quickly when things go wrong. However, the road to creating followership means that when things go awry, the manager is the first to accept responsibility. Then the leader assumes the role to bring the team together to embark upon effective problem solving. A boss works to leave coworkers with the sense that he, she or they are always, without fail, the smartest person in the room. On the other hand, the manager seeks to build followership, carries a level of genuine humility that broadcasts to the team: "I – and therefore we – simply cannot be successful without each of us playing our part and being the best we can be."

As an example of how an aligned team would look and act, a sports coach instructs the team toward how to win in a game. The coach provides ongoing feedback before the game, throughout and after. The team is focused on what they need to do to win. It is the same in business. A manager must clearly define what a win would look like, and how each player must contribute. Then they must coach on a consistent basis and provide ongoing commentary to the individuals on the team. Thus, the team knows how they are doing from their coach's perspective. When obstacles arise, the leader must continue to focus and inspire the team to win.

Each of us has blind spots. To fill in the missing information, managers must engage in fruitful conversations on a consistent schedule to support each person on their team. The dialogue should be two-way, so each person is gaining insight into their potential blind spots. This continues to align teams focused on that which is most important.

Sue Seamon, Business Owner, weighs in by stating:

"Always share the "bigger picture" with your team. Each member needs to understand the value they're bringing to the overall strategy, not just their individual contribution."

While this seems like common sense, it is not common practice. Time and time again, I have witnessed employees stating they had no idea what the goals of the organization were. Furthermore, they were unaware of the department goals. That lack of awareness leads to employees simply doing their job rather than owning the results that needed to be achieved. It's called "check the box" syndrome and it shows up when employees are not engaged.

One way to engage your employees is to communicate and interpret the goals that need to be accomplished by the team and by the individuals. Then the employees can take ownership for those results.

Self-Reflection Questions:

- Do you know what a win would look like for your organization? Have you communicated that with each of your team members?
- Do you know what a win would like for each of your employees? Do they know?
- Do you meet with them in a two-way dialogue to reduce their blind spots and yours?
- You have an employee you suspect may be disengaged. How do you handle this?

11

Be a Mentor, Find a Mentor

"My favorite mentor unleashed my passions, channeled my energy, guided my growth and encouraged my success."
~Anna Letitia Cook

More and more organizations are realizing the benefits of having mentors and/or coaches to help develop their people. One large organization, with which I worked, sends internal employees to become certified as coaches in addition to handling their regular position. In our meeting, these coaches verbalized their excitement to have this unique challenge. They did not see it as extra work but as an opportunity to expand what they would normally do plus learn a new skill. This investment sends the message to the employees that they are important, and their development is critical to the success of the organization.

Smaller organizations may not yet have this type of initiative, but that does not mean you cannot pursue the option of having a coach or mentor yourself. As a matter of fact, although many organizations outsource coaches, you do not need a structure in place to ask someone who may be more tenured, experienced, older, or wiser in your company to be your mentor. Set the goals up front. Structure your relationship with clear boundaries. Parameters to consider are confidentiality, safety (no retaliation, retribution etc.), and time investment.

Determine what is important for you to learn. Why are you seeking this person to mentor you? What is the outcome you hope to achieve? The more specific you are, the more you will gain from your mentor/mentee relationship. If it is successful, you may even want to share your success with HR so they can determine the viability of going companywide with a similar program.

Another option is to seek an external coach. While there are a wide variety of coaches, the typical format used is Google Meet Video, Zoom, or phone so you are not limited only to coaches in your area. Choose a coach who is certified and experienced in your specialty. There are several types of coaches in a variety of areas including, health and wellness, mindfulness, neuroscience, strategic, leadership and non-profit coaches. While there may be many more than this list, determine what would most benefit you based on your need and search for that type.

International Coach Federation (https://coachingfederation.org), the globally recognized coach credentialed organization, has a website that can help you locate a coach that specializes in your area. The benefit to having a coach is that you can continue to deepen your own self-reflection. I call coaches the truth mirrors. They can assist in uncovering the root of self-sabotage, self-doubt, and other areas that may be in the way of leading strong. I have found it beneficial to have a third party help me to recognize that which I failed to see myself. That 30,000-foot view is valuable. Unless we seek outside support, we often miss opportunities for growth.

The best way to gain an understanding of other people's roles is to mentor them. By helping others, we tend to see themes that can be applicable to what we are experiencing. We can see what they do not see, their blind spots.

During a coaching session I was leading, my client's experiences were exactly poignant in my life. It was easy for me to see the answers for her, while I had been struggling with my own answers for me. It was not until I heard her detail her conclusions that I realized I needed to do the same work.

In karate, we take classes to learn. But in order to master the art, one must teach. In the same way, you learn when you mentor others. In helping others with their challenges, we may then see solutions to our own similar problems.

Self-Reflection Questions:

- What would you gain from having a coach or mentor?
- What would someone else gain from having YOU as a mentor?
- Are there any beliefs that may prevent you from accepting a coach?

12

Confrontation Does Not Equal Battle

"To not confront poor execution and behavior is to endorse it. To not reinforce good execution and behavior is to extinguish it."
~Dick Vermeil

Many organizations struggle with communication. In fact, every organization with which I have worked has had some form of communication challenge.

In a group of managers, a gentleman commented about the "nice" culture his organization had. Because people felt they had a familial environment, they wanted to protect each other to not hurt one another's feelings. "They weren't willing to state negatives," he continued, "because they liked and valued one another." The group agreed with his assessment, placing value on their relationships. He admitted there was a cost since they were missing deadlines and opportunities to avoid "failures." Quite frankly, they were in a very reactive mode because they couldn't acknowledge their challenges. From his perspective, they didn't want to sacrifice their value of "nice" and respect for one another. He equated being nice with not being able to raise issues that could be construed as negative or confrontational. Thus, they kept quiet instead of potentially threatening that value. This was perpetuated in their culture.

We avoid tough conversations because we believe saying something will hurt someone's feelings or threaten the work they have done. My strong belief is that we have to approach honest communication differently.

Instead of looking for the negative, highlight the positive. That does not mean sugarcoating the issues, simply intend to build your colleagues up, not tear them down. When we criticize, we say, "You speak so much in meetings that you dominate the time and prevent others from sharing." When we restate that in a useful fashion we might say, "I appreciate when you are really considerate of your words before you speak. You really offer a lot of value when you do that." If we look for opportunities to help build one another up, then we are not looking for opportunities to criticize.

A confrontation can be an opportunity to learn. I have approached many "awkward conversations" with the thought of how can I learn from this and how can I help? Confrontation does not mean we are going into battle.

It can include a variety of approaches: we have a difference of opinion or we view things through different filters. We need to communicate with one another to share those perspectives. I approach these conversations considering how my words may impact the other person first. Then, I determine if their reaction would direct us toward a mutual beneficial outcome.

Sometimes we need to deliver information that may potentially hurt feelings. Use the time to creatively talk about what it is and what can be learned from it. If we lay the foundation that "failing fast" is okay as long as we learn from it, we are building a stronger foundation for people to thrive. If your team member has a fear of the consequences of failure, that will stifle creativity, innovation, and a willingness to be honest. The channels of communication must be clear and upfront for the highest level of success to occur. If you model that for your people, then you send the non-verbal message that it's okay to talk about the tough subjects without negative consequences.

For example, I was at a meeting where each of us were presenting over two days. When it became my turn to present, I moved in front of the room, and my manager left the room. I noticed it, because I was the only one for whom he was absent.

I started getting upset and felt disrespected. I wondered why he left during my presentation. I caught myself going down a negative path. I decided I would allow him to interpret for me instead of creating his rationale for him.

The next day I asked him, "What experience do you think you created for me when you left the room as I was about to present?" I was not angry or accusing. He was so grateful I inquired. He said, "Please let me interpret what happened." He shared that an emergency with an employee occurred right at that moment, and he was pulled out to handle it. He apologized and said he had really wanted to see my presentation.

That would not have been the story I would have created if I had been left to my own devices. Instead, we engaged in a healthy conversation.

Confrontation doesn't have to be offensive. We can approach communication with positive intention. If our plan is to vent angry feelings, then our subjects will feel that. The conversation will not go well. It takes self-reflection and the ability to ask for what we truly desire the outcome to be. This is being an intentional leader.

Self-Reflection Questions:

- Are you holding back where you could be more truthful?
- In what way could you be more straightforward?
- How would you like to be confronted?
- What would move the conversation forward?
- If you had a tough conversation and felt accused or demeaned, how could you approach this person so that you achieve a win-win situation?

13

Manage Time or It Will Manage You

"It is not enough to be busy...The question is: what are we busy about?"
~Henry David Thoreau

If you are driven to succeed in business, you may also believe you need to work hard, come in early/stay late in order to prove your value as an employee. Because many want to move quickly up the ladder of success, the need to establish yourself upfront is important. The key to longevity is to find the balance between work and your personal life.

Many organizations have prioritized health & wellness as a

part of their strategic initiatives for their annual plans. They realize that employees are not useful if they are burned out. Burnout results in high turnover. Yet, the need to accomplish a tremendous amount with only a few resources is the reality of many organizations. Therefore, you must take responsibility for establishing your balance. This is even more important for employees who work at home remotely. It's difficult to set boundaries when your office is now your living room. As an intentional leader, we must have empathy for that challenge with ourselves and with those who work for us.

Recently, I was working with a leader of an HR team who felt a tremendous responsibility to be in-service to others. As a leader of the HR department, she felt job satisfaction when she witnessed employees thriving. One of her colleagues, a leader of the sales division, would frequently ask her to "help" him. This usually meant, "Will you create my Excel spreadsheets?" He didn't know how to do it. And since she kept saying "yes" to the work, he requested she do more. The challenge for her was to say no to him and communicate that she felt he should know how to do this as a leader.

I shared a perspective with her that was from the heart. I suggested she enabled him by doing his work, and that she may not always be around when he needs it. By her wanting to please him and help him, she was robbing him of learning how to do a necessary part of his job. We discussed her holding him accountable to learn, and she felt she would be punishing him by refusing. So, she continued to shy away from saying "no." We reframed the situation and viewed it through the intentional leader approach. Thus, she was able to embrace her next steps. By allowing him the opportunity to learn Excel to build important spreadsheets that he will use in every role moving forward, she would be giving him the opportunity to gain a valuable skill. As a result, she held him accountable in a positive manner. This also freed up her time to manage and accomplish her responsibilities thus she was more productive.

Manage your time efficiently and intentionally. This way you can include time for good nutrition, exercise, and a social life. When the scale is out of balance, you are not able to give your best. (See my book *Unleash Your Power* to learn more about balance and fulfillment).

Self-Reflection Questions:

- What areas of your life are neglected?
- Where are you needing to spend time and energy to have more fulfillment?
- You have several open positions and the work is overwhelming. One of your employees is a "clock watcher" and completes bare minimum. Another employee works until late at night and does the lion share of the communal work. How do you handle this?

14

Change & Lead Strong

"Leadership is about making others better as a result of your presence and making sure that the impact lasts in your absence."
~Sheryl Sandberg

Model what you want others to do. Talk your talk. Follow through on your word or interpret for people when you need to adjust the plan. Respect those who work for you and around you. These are simple ideas and yet so often I hear managers lack one or several of these elements.

Change is not easy. When asked, many of us say "oh yes, I embrace change", but when change comes without notice, we resist. Life will forever change. How will you react when change is upon you? As you read some of the strategies in this book to increase your people skills, do you try, fail and give up? Do you judge yourself for not doing it perfectly? I have learned to lean in to change and allow space for failing, succeeding, or just meeting my goals. I usually do a post-mortem so to speak and look for what I would do differently to improve in the future. But I do so from love, not fear. I do not tear myself down for my failures anymore. It just makes things worse. It is a common trap. But it is so detrimental. We are human and we will forever make mistakes. The question is, "then what?" How will you handle yourself when you do not live up to your own expectation? By allowing yourself space to not have to be perfect, you are also modeling for your people *perfect* is never the bar. "The best you can" is always a better bar. When you miss, learn from it. Even better, share some of those misses with your team so they can learn how to do the same. Self-compassion leads to higher resilience.

When asked what advice you would give new managers, Sue Seamon adds:

"A successful team is like an orchestra. Each member contributes skill and passion to the overall performance. The manager is simply the conductor".

- Maintain your sense of humor. Be able to laugh at yourself.
- Listen to all viewpoints before making a decision.
- Acknowledge to your team that their opinion counts.
- Foster individual and team engagement.

- Assign hi-potential employees to a mentor to gain new and different perspectives.
- Help build an employee's self-esteem.
- Meet regularly with each of your direct reports. Discuss progress on company goals and development goals.
- When possible, provide a stage for individual contributors to present to senior managers.

A new managerial role can seem overwhelming. There are constants in business that you can expect to encounter. One of them is change, the other is uncertainty. Priorities may constantly change leaving you wondering what you should deem most important. Differing personalities within the organization can be a challenge. Perhaps you have people who are passive aggressive, and you are needing to decipher the code to figure out where they are and how to proceed? All of these are potential triggers that can set us off at any time. The more we are aware of our triggers, the more we can thoughtfully respond (rather than thoughtlessly reacting) in an appropriate, non-emotive fashion. This is the behavior of a self-aware intentional leader.

An important foundation to being a manager is to have the courage to do what is right and to be fearless to walk on rough roads ahead. The principles in this guide will provide you with fundamentals to develop your inner intentional leader. They are not sequential, but all play a role in successful leadership. Be willing to receive thoughts and comments from your team on how your leadership has impacted them. Consider it a win when people are willing to be honest with you. This will expedite your growth as a successful intentional leader.

www.ingramcontent.com/pod-product-compliance
Lightning Source LLC
Chambersburg PA
CBHW071911070526
44583CB00016B/1946